Make a New Friend in Jesus

PassAlong Arch® Books help you share Jesus with friends close to you and with children all around the world!

When you've enjoyed this story, pass it along to a friend. When your friend is finished, mail this book to the address below. Concordia Gospel Outreach promises to deliver your book to a boy or girl somewhere in the world to help him or her learn about Jesus.

Myself

My name _____

My address _____

_____

My PassAlong Friend

My name _____

My address _____

_____

When you're ready to give your PassAlong Arch® Book to a new friend who doesn't know about Jesus, mail it to

Concordia Gospel Outreach
3547 Indiana Avenue
St. Louis, MO 63118

PassAlong Series

God's Good Creation
Noah's Floating Zoo
Baby Moses' River Ride
Moses and the Freedom Journey
Journey to the Promised Land
David and the Dreadful Giant
Jonah's Fishy Adventure
Daniel in the Dangerous Den
Baby Jesus, Prince of Peace
Jesus Stills the Storm
Jesus and Jairus' Little Girl
Jesus' Big Picnic
Jesus and the Little Children
Jesus and the Grumpy Little Man
God's Easter Plan
Peter and the Biggest Birthday

Copyright © 1995 Concordia Publishing House
3558 S. Jefferson Avenue, St. Louis, MO 63118-3968
Manufactured in the United States of America

1 2 3 4 5 6 7 8 9 10   04 03 02 01 00 99 98 97 96 95

Journey to the Promised Land

Exodus 15:23–Joshua 4:24 for Children

Carol Greene

Illustrated by Michelle Dorenkamp

SAINT LOUIS

God had set His people free from Egyptland
With outstretched arm and mighty hand.
Safe across the sea, they sang their songs
    of praise.
Then on they marched for three long days.

"I don't miss Egypt one bit!"

Marching through the wilderness is not
     much fun.
God's people sweltered in the sun.
"Water's what we need," they croaked,
     their voices rough,
But what they found was bitter stuff.

Moses cried to God, and God said,
     "Throw that wood
Into the water. Now it's good."
Good indeed it was to throats so dry
     and sore,
And then God's people marched
     some more.

"There are times when *nothing* is better than water."

When they reached a desert by the name
    of Sin,
They started to complain again.
"This place is too rough and there's no
    food to find.
We're going to starve!" they wailed and
    whined.

Then God spoke to Moses. "I have heard
    their cry.
Each morn I'll send bread from the sky.
In the evening quail will come, and
    they'll have meat.
They'll always have enough to eat."

"God's people called the bread manna."

Months went by, and every time a problem
   came,
God helped His people just the same.
He conquered all their enemies and kept
   them strong.
But still God's folk sometimes did
   wrong.

When they camped in Sinai at the
   mountain's base,
God told Moses, "In this place,
I will speak to you and let the people hear,
But don't let anyone come near."

"What will God say?"

On the third day, Moses led the people out.
Smoke wrapped the mountain round
about.
Lightning flashed and trumpet shrieked.
The smoke rose higher.
Then God the Lord appeared in fire.

"I am God, your Lord, the one who set
you free,
And you shall have no gods but Me.
You shall not make idols for your prayers
and praise,
Nor use My name in sinful ways.

"Who'd want an idol when they have God?"

Set aside the seventh day, for it is Mine.
Let honor for your parents shine.
Do not kill. Do not commit adultery,
Nor steal, nor speak untruthfully.

"Do not long for things that don't belong
    to you,"
God said. The people shook clear through.
"Moses, we will die. You speak to God instead,
Then tell us later what He said."

"If people follow those rules, they'll be happy."

So Moses took his helper, Joshua by name,
And climbed the mountain to the flame.
Moses' brother Aaron was in charge below.
The days dragged by, so long, so slow.

Then at last the people went to Aaron's tent.
"We don't know where that Moses went.
But we need a god right now and we
     have none.
Please, Aaron, will you make us one?"

"What?"

What a thing to ask! But Aaron didn't laugh.
Instead, he made a golden calf.
"That's our god!" the people said. They
   held a feast
And danced and sang before the beast.

God knew what they'd done, and how
   His anger flared!
But Moses begged, "Let them be spared.
You have led them this far with Your
   mighty hand.
Oh, lead them to the Promised Land!"

"I don't blame God for being angry!"

Once again God listened, once again
        forgave.
But back at camp how Moses raved!
He broke the stones that told God's laws,
        and then he turned,
And, raging still, the calf he burned.

"Who is for the Lord?" he cried, and some
        said, "I!"
"Well, those who aren't must surely die."
Finally, the people journeyed on again,
But they were far from done with sin.

"Imagine pretending that a metal cow is your god!"

One day, God told Moses to send spies ahead.
"The Promised Land is near," He said.
When the spies came back, some said the
        land was fine.
But others started in to whine.

"People there are huge. Why, they could
        smush us flat!"
They moaned, and when the folks
        heard that,
How they groused and grumbled. "Let's
        go back," they said,
"To Egypt. God must want us dead."

"Can you believe they still don't trust God?"

Joshua had spied and now he cried out, "No!
The land is good. I tell you so.
Trust in God, you people. He is on our side."
But still the people quaked inside.

"How long will they doubt Me?" God told
        Moses then.
"Each doubt insults Me. So again
Back into the wilderness I'll have them go
To wander forty years. Tell them so."

"You really messed up this time, folks."

Forty years is very long to walk and wait.
The people's hearts grew hard with hate.
They said ugly things of God, and Moses too,
A stupid, sinful thing to do.

God sent fiery snakes with poison in each bite.
Again the people shook with fright.
"Moses, talk to God," they pled.
　　"These snakes can kill."
And Moses sighed, "All right. I will."

"I do not
like
fiery snakes."

Make a snake and put it on a pole of wood,"
God said. "A bitten person should
Look at it, and then that person's life
   I'll save."
God had not changed. He still forgave.

Time went by and Moses soon must die,
   so he
Climbed a mountain. God said, "See?
That's the Promised Land there on
   the other side.
Now, come with Me." And Moses died.

"Moses was very old and tired by then."

Then God said to Joshua, "The journey's past.
Come, lead My people home at last."
Straight into the Jordan River marched
the priests.
At God's command, its flowing ceased.

God had made a path through water
long before.
Now He'd made a path once more.
Through the journey He had every
promise kept.
He *was* their God. And so they stepped . . .

"God is so good to His people."

Down into the river, to the other shore,
Thousands of them, score on score.
There it lay, God's answer to so many
prayers,
The Promised Land. And it was theirs.

"I guess God loves them a *lot!*"